The Namer

How do I find my true identity?

The Namer

How do I find my true identity?

Matt Rawlins

Amuzement Publications

Dedication

This book is dedicated to my wife Celia. Her beauty, love and friendship mean the world to me.

Acknowledgement

I could not have done this without the help of a small writers group and the fearless leader, Sandi Tompkins. She is a brilliant editor and writer.

The Namer

Now the LORD God had formed out of the ground all the beasts of the field and all the birds of the air. He brought them to the man to see what he would name them; and whatever the man called each living creature, that was its name (Gen. 2:19).

Prologue

As God is, He spoke.

His creative word only brought forth that which was an expression of Himself. This is all eternity knew or would ever know had He not taken a risk. His first risk was speaking forth finite beings He named angels. They would be part of His Kingdom. They would share in His Glory.

A group of them decided it was not enough to share in His Glory. They wanted to take His Glory and make it their own. The leader of the rebel pack changed his name from Lucifer to Satan. Other angels joined him and gave themselves new names. Some of those names are Infirmity, Disease, Anger, Jealousy, Liar, Hatred, Strife and Works. Others names are Deception, Vanity, Despair,

Destroyer, Impurity, Stupor, Division, Unbelief, Timidity.

These rebel angels were evicted from the city of God, but for the first time in the history of the universe, God's creative expression, the rebel angels, misused their ability to name the world. Their words were not in line with reality.

One would have thought that this would have so pained *The Pure One* that He would not take the risk again. But as *The Wise One* is far above our thoughts, so are His ways. He took another risk. This risk was in creating mankind. He spoke forth our world and then formed a handful of dust, created man and woman and breathed into them the breath of life.

* * *

Adam and Eve awoke in a new world. They stared at the splendor around them. They soaked in its beauty. Colors abounded with each turn of their head.

Sounds came from every direction.
Their senses stirred with each scent,
sight and noise as fresh feelings washed
over them. Each moment carried a new
experience like none other.

Eve turned to God *The Sovereign One*
and asked, "You have made all this?"
The Living Word replied, "Yes, I spoke
it all into existence. I have created it for
you."

"You have made all this? For us?" Eve
asked.

"Yes, it is yours. However, I have not
finished it. You must do that."

"What do you mean? How could you,
The Perfect One, not finish something?"
Adam asked.

The All Knowing One replied, "*I AM* the
Creator of all life, and you are made in
my image as my son and daughter. In
your world, I have left creation incomplete that you may exhibit my image in
you."

"How are we to do that?" Adam questioned.

The Author of Life replied, "*I AM* the Source of all life. I have spoken all things into existence except you. I have not spoken, but breathed you into existence. I have given you life by giving you a part of myself. My breath in you is my word unspoken. My breath in you is my gift to you. Your will and faith will release that gift. My breath, through your spoken word, will identify and define your world confirming each element of creation's meaning and value."

The Humble One waited for a moment, "I have made you in My image. Your words have power. You may speak forth out of My breath that is in you and finish creation by naming it. I have not named any of the animals of the field or birds of the air. Although I have given each animal an identity, I have not given it a name. That I have left for you to do."

"How shall we name them?" Adam asked.

"You must examine their uniqueness, their beauty, their life. As you watch, you will find names that express the places I have given them in this world. The names you choose will be the final demonstration of their identity."

"This naming of creation will be an expression of your authority over it. For he who names something has authority over what he names," *The Wise One* declared. "The only boundary I put on you is that you must not rename yourselves. For you are made in my image, thus, I have called you my son and my daughter. I have already named you. Your place is already set. If you rename yourselves, you will die."

* * *

Time passed as Adam and Eve explored and began to name the inhabitants of their world. They carefully watched each animal and recognized its uniqueness and then gave each one a name.

They were validating and honoring the beauty of creation and the unique relationship each aspect of creation would have to the world around them.

Days passed like minutes as they reveled in the sheer joy of it all. Yet, unexpectedly, out of nowhere, came an adversary.

The woman heard a sound behind her and turned to see what it was. This creature was not like anything else she had seen. It was strangely beautiful.

"I bring greetings my lady," it began.

"I'm sorry, have I not named you?"

"Oh, thank you, but I have already given myself a name," it replied, "Who are you?"

"I am Eve, the daughter of *The Sovereign Creator*."

"What have you been doing?" it asked.

"I have been naming the animals," Eve proclaimed.

"Is that all?" it responded as if bored.

"Is that all? What do you mean? I have known a deep and growing joy in these last days. Who would want anything else?"

"Ahh yes, I understand, I greatly admire your gift for naming. I think you are doing a brilliant job," it stated through a stifled yawn.

"Thank you," Eve responded.

"I just think it is underused," it added.

Eve turned to look at it carefully and asked, "What do you mean?"

"Well," it started, "You are naming animals. How have they responded to you?"

"They are excited and have great pleasure in our naming them."

"So there is great pleasure in being named?" it inquired.

"Oh, yes," Eve replied, " it seems the highest honor I can give creation."

"I would agree with that," it encouraged, "all creation must seek out its highest place of honor."

Eve asked, "What do you mean seek out its highest place of honor? Our job is to recognize the honor that the Creator gave it."

"Oh, just to recognize something's honor that is already there is not the best use of your gift," it seductively whispered. "Anyone can do that. When I mentioned earlier that your wonderful gift is underused, I meant that a true namer can make things greater by giving them a greater name."

"How can that be?" Eve questioned.

"Hmm, let me think. Let's use you as an example."

"OK."

"You have named yourself, right?"

"No, I cannot," Eve retorted, "*My Father* has told me that I cannot name myself. He alone is wise enough to name me."

"Ahh, you have the gift of naming, but cannot name yourself?" It paused, "Think of the pleasure each of the animals had in your naming them. That pleasure and more can be yours. All you need to do is name yourself."

Eve stated, "I cannot do that for *The Sovereign Namer* has told me I can name all things but myself. If I name myself, I will die."

"You surely will not die! You said you are his daughter! I think *The All Powerful One* has given you the identity of a child. Did you know that you could have the same identity He has? Would you rob yourself of the joy you so freely gave to those you named?"

"But why would I rename myself?"

"You would have the same joy He had in naming you. You will be like Him."

"I am not sure I see the joy of renaming myself when he has told me not to," Eve pondered out loud.

"But maybe He told you not to, just to test you to see if you would take the risk on your own."

"I don't think He wants me to take that kind of risk."

"Wouldn't that be the greatest gift He could give? If He told you to do it then you wouldn't be doing it on your own? It would still be Him telling you what to do. The greatest naming must be the risk you take to name yourself. What greater joy could you have than the freedom to name yourself?"

"It is still not clear to me what would be the joy of naming something He told me not to name?" Eve asked.

"If you named yourself, you would then have power over yourself. You know that power is given to the one who names something. The joy would be that you are the greatest namer because only the greatest namers can name themselves."

"Ah, and there you are wrong. I think He gave me boundaries because there are some things that are beyond my ability to understand. Thus, I cannot clearly identify them. What if His identity was so great, so wonderful, so far beyond my ability to comprehend, that when He gave me His identity and called me His child, I could not fully understand it and would have all eternity to learn to define myself as I learn to understand Him. Wouldn't that give me a wonderful, intimate relationship with Him?"

It laughingly mocked her, then hastily responded, "Only those who cut themselves off from the boundaries that have been imposed on them will be great. True namers know no boundaries. All others are just copies with no power to truly create."

The hollow words seemed to bounce off her. No bother, he would say it again in a thousand different ways at a thousand different times if need be.

The conversation took a turn for the worse as mankind reached for the power to name ourselves and experienced the knowledge of evil.

* * *

"Adam, what have we done? What do I call these feelings that I am experiencing? I feel exposed, ashamed, vulnerable and dirty. I am terrified," Eve *the deceived one* said as she gathered leaves to cover herself.

Adam *the defiant one* hesitated and then finally responded, "We have rebelled from Our Creator. His breath in us is gone. I realize now, it is like the scent of a flower rebelling from the flower. Our declared freedom to name our self is our death."

They heard the familiar sound of footsteps and froze. God was coming. For the first time, Adam and Eve were terrified, they ran into the woods and hid behind a tree.

What would the Sovereign Namer name them now that they had rebelled from His family?

The Broken One called out to Adam, "Where are you?"

Adam's voice whimpered from the trees, "I heard you coming and I was afraid because I was naked; so I hid myself."

The Loving One asked, "Who told you that you were naked? Have you rebelled against my authority and renamed yourself?"

Adam turned his gifting against *The Just One* and named Him and the woman as the guilty ones, "The woman, whom you gave me," he hesitated to make the point stronger, "was deceived and renamed herself, and I reluctantly joined her."

* * *

Upon their decision, and our decisions, our world is what it is.

Now, all mankind has inherited the challenge of this gift gone astray, and the questions that it raises.

Naming ourselves is no easy task as our identity is not in our power to understand. It is like being stuck in the dark, with no ability to generate light, and yet accepting the responsibility to see.

Prologue Two

Who are we?

Is a name an identity?

The ability to name our world was meant to be like a beautifully colored feather mantle or shawl placed on a king or queen. The mantle doesn't make them a king or queen, but it distinguishes them, adds beauty and honor and validates the glory of who they are. Our ability to name was meant to add beauty and honor to us, confirming our role as image bearers and rulers over the world.

What did we do with this gift?

We turned it on ourselves. We tried to give ourselves a greater name. This brought great pain and suffering for all of us. Now, the ability to name does not confirm our true identity, instead, we use it to hide with. Not something to honor but something to hide under. The mantle has become a cloak.

Some examples may help. With a real stretch of the imagination, the Klingons from Star Trek had a special device on their war ship that when turned on, made the ship invisible. It was called a cloaking device. With its use they became invisible. On a much simpler level, sometimes at the beach or by a pool, ladies wear large T-shirts that go down to their knees. Painted on the T-shirt is a figure of a skinny woman in a bathing suit. The person wearing it is often shaped differently. The fun illusion of the T-shirt and the cloaking device on a ship are similar ways of how we use our ability to name. We hide our true identity by trying to name ourselves or cloak ourselves differently.

Our ability to name is now used to protect us, hide us, or to put on an image we want others to see, rather than express our true identity.

Part I

Chapter I

Saul arose from bed as on other day
and ate breakfast. His father entered the
kitchen and asked, "Saul, have you seen
the donkeys?"

"They weren't in my room, I haven't
seen anything this morning."

"Well, they are lost and the servants
said they haven't been in the field where
they usually feed. Take one of the servants and find the donkeys."

"OK, I'll find them," Saul mumbled.

Saul and his servant headed out into the
field trying to look for any clues. There
were none. Hours turned into days
and after many miles of travel they still
could not find the donkeys. Saul now
wondered whether his father would

worry about him instead of the donkeys. In a last ditch effort to get help, they decided to see a prophet who was close by and ask if he knew where the donkeys were.

The prophet's name was Samuel. He knew something Saul would have never guessed. Saul was to be the new king. The people of Israel wanted a new identity. They didn't want God as their model anymore.

God brought Saul to the prophet, through the lost donkeys, to tell Saul that he was going to be the new King for Israel. Saul was to give them a new expression of God in their midst.

"Prophet, may I ask you a question?" Saul asked Samuel.

"Please go ahead," Samuel replied.

Saul began, "I have lost my donkeys and I have searched all over for them. I have some silver to pay for your help. Can you seek the Lord and tell me where my donkeys are?"

Samuel declared, "Your donkeys are safe at home. I have another message for you from the Lord. You are the one that all of Israel desires."

Saul gasped, "I'm what? You've got to be kidding! Did you know that I am from the smallest tribe of Israel, and my family is the least significant of all the families in the tribe. Surely you mistake me for someone else?"

Samuel shook his head and replied, "You are a handsome young man. You stand head and shoulders above all others in our country. The people desire a strong, handsome King and the Lord has chosen you to fill that role."

With that, the anointing oil was poured on Saul's head and Samuel explained the miracles God would provide to confirm it to him.

"Saul, it shall be when these miracles come to pass, do for yourself what the occasion requires; for God is with you.

Then, in seven days, wait until I come to you and show you what you should do next."

Chapter II

Saul turned from talking to Samuel,
stunned by the turn of events. All he
wanted was to find his father's donkeys
and Samuel told him he was to be king.
Me, small and insignificant Saul? King?
the words ran through his mind.

He felt like weights were dropping from
him. The heaviness and pressure of his
insignificance seemed to be lifting. He
felt so light and free he could almost
float away. Then he heard *The Sovereign
Namer* whisper to him, "You are loved.
You are chosen. You are to bear my image. I will be with you." He wanted to
turn around to see who had said it, but
he knew. It was God at work in him.

Saul was to express God's identity before the people. For a moment he saw
creation around him for the first time

and realized his place in it. He realized his gifting as a namer. He could see, feel and hear the world around him and based on this, he could identify the world because he had God's breath in him and bore God's image.

Each of the events Samuel had foretold came about. Saul met the men who said the donkeys were safe, gifts were given to him and when he came to the hill and saw a group of prophets and he stood among them, he himself started to prophesy. *Yes, God was with him.*

Saul walked home stunned. *How could this be?* he wondered.

He finally arrived home and Saul's uncle was the first to appear. Sensing something different in Saul, he asked, "What has happened? Please tell me what Samuel said to you."

Saul *the anointed, the beloved one*, decided to tell his uncle about Samuel and his anointing him as the new king. Just as he was about to begin, Saul looked into his uncle's eyes and he saw it. His uncle's questioning stare of insignificance and unbelief was there. Saul *the anointed one,* hesitated. He felt caught between what God has just done and his own personal experiences and feelings of insignificance. It seemed so much safer and simpler to trust his own and his families view then God's. After a brief moment, he said to his uncle, "Samuel just told us the donkeys were okay." But Saul did not tell him about being the new king. His uncle would not have believed him.

* * *

The greatest miracle was that *The Truthful One* changed Saul's heart. He gave him a new heart. In the language of this story, He revealed to Saul his true identity. God stepped in and gave Saul a new opportunity.

An opportunity? What does that mean? We have lost God's perspective. We have become accustomed to living and struggling in a fallen world and cannot possibly see ourselves as we are created to be. It is impossible for us to comprehend reality, unless God reveals it to us. *The Gracious One* gave Saul an opportunity for life and revealed his identity to him.

God gave him a complete identity it just wasn't fulfilled yet, for we each must play a part in the process of life. He gives us a start by answering our question about who we are. When Saul left the prophet and God showed him miracles to prove what He was going to do, He changed his identity to give him a new start.

The Long Suffering One can give us a new identity but he can't force us to keep it. That is up to us. An identity is not a thing that can be replaced and then left alone. It is a living, growing 'life' that must be cared for. Here is the key, just as all life must take in food to survive and develop, so we must feed our identity in order for it to grow and survive. That is the part we are to play. It is out of the experiences of our existence that we provide the nourishment for it to develop.

What did Saul feed his identity?

Although God gave Saul a new identity, he fed it a diet that starved it out, or changed it back to what it was before. For, our identity grows out of the thoughts, beliefs and experiences we nourish it with. Saul wouldn't accept the revelation God offered. He only supported it on the provisions from his own ideas and experiences and that is what killed the new identity God gave him.

The food God offered — and the only food as Image Bearers that will nourish our identity and establish our true name — is understanding who God is.

Revelation of who He is, is the only food we were made to live on. Anything else will starve and eventually kill us. If we will not embrace the only source of food we were made to live on, then we will have to accept the consequences of trying to feed ourselves: death. If we pursue and embrace revelation of His

Goodness and Greatness through humility, then His Image can grow and become strong in us.

Chapter III

To formalize the process of selecting
a king for the people, Samuel called
a gathering of all the tribes and drew
lots to see who *The Patient One* would
choose to be king. After the lots were
drawn, Saul was the one chosen.

"Where is Saul?" Samuel asked.

The people began to look among themselves and a common voice arose, "He is
not here."

Samuel asked God where he was and
heard these odd words, "He is hiding
himself among the baggage."

Samuel mumbled, "That is a funny
place for a king to be."

Saul *the anointed, the insignificant one,* lay hidden among the carts in the storage area.

Saul wondered at the events that led him there. *How could I have let this happen? I didn't ask for this! They will see me as my Uncle saw me. They will ask to see who I am, and I am afraid of the answer. When they see me the way I see myself, they will know I am not enough.*

He heard the people running toward him and fear gripped him as he cowered lower to protect himself. The people took him from there and when they saw his height and how handsome he was they shouted in unison, "Long live the king!"

Chapter IV

Saul had a problem that all of us can identify with. Although God had given him a new identity, he still had thoughts, beliefs, painful experiences and memories from his past struggles to try to name himself that he had to overcome. These experiences and thoughts battled in his mind. Who should he trust? Should he trust what he felt and the experiences of his life? Or, should he trust what God said about him?

In the world in which we are born, it is a difficult, but common challenge, faced by almost everyone.

How did Saul deal with these challenges?

Saul's earliest and strongest experiences to his questions about himself came through the name given by his family and culture. He was from the smallest tribe, the Benjamites. His family was the least of all of the families of the Benjamites.

Simple logic in naming himself sounded something like this. "I am from the least significant family, of the smallest tribe, therefore, who I am is small and insignificant."

This creates a major problem for Saul. For how God sees him is in direct opposition to how he knows himself. When he looks inside, he sees a lifetime of experiences and feelings and sees himself as small and insignificant. With the feelings he has felt his whole life, he decides to trust himself over God. After all, it seemed only right that he knew himself better than anyone else could.

Saul's own thoughts and feelings overwhelm him and his response is to hide among the baggage at the thought that everyone will see him and honor him.

He is confused. How can a small and insignificant one be king?
He is bewildered. How can he be made in the image of God?

He knows he doesn't deserve the honor because of the feelings deep inside himself that he has accepted as reality.

He hears God wooing him to accept his true identity, but he pushes it aside and argues that it can't be true. He will decide what is real and what his name should be.

God has a plan for him that is bigger than the name Saul has for himself. God has an identity for him that is far greater than any identity that he can find on earth.

Chapter V

Saul *the anointed, the insignificant one,* awoke and sat up in bed. It was the same nightmare again. He wiped the sweat off of his forehead and lay back down. His mind struggled to understand the nightmare. *I crave the light to find who I am. So I walk into the light and the shadow thrown from me is small and insignificant. Those that see me laugh and mock me. 'Such a big and beautiful man throws such a small and insignificant shadow.' I turn to flee and the only place to flee is into darkness. It is only there that there is no shadow, but in the darkness I am lost.*

Saul rolled over as if to turn away from the shadow. *If I live in the darkness, I am lost and alone for no one can see me. How can I understand who I am? Is it through what others say? Is it through my past experiences with my family and culture? How*

43

can God love me when He knows what I am
on the inside? How can others accept me
when I know what I am deep inside?

What was the shadow?

In the fallen world our forefathers have
passed on to us, the shadow was Saul's
own image of himself. It was his feelings of loneliness and of being small and
insignificant. It was his own answer to
the questions about himself that he was
never supposed to ask. Saul's shadow
was the painful lie that his own name
was small and insignificant. In our fallen
world, sadly, it is a painful, but common
image.

Chapter VI

A small neighboring rebel group surrounded the town of Jabesh-gilead, a town in Israel. They arrogantly declared, "To prove we are your masters, we will put out the right eye of everyone in the town if you don't surrender."

The leaders of Jabesh-gilead replied, "Please give us seven days to think about your offer. We will send our messengers for help throughout our land. If no one comes to save us, then we will surrender to you."

They agreed and the wait began.

Saul *the anointed, the insignificant one,* hears about it and God's Spirit comes mightily upon him and he is enraged. He cuts up his oxen into small pieces and sends the pieces to all of Israel saying, "So shall it be done to the oxen of those who do not come to help."

Dread falls upon the people and they rally to join their new king.

A battle is fought and they win their first victory. A kingdom is established. The taste of victory is sweet. The people rejoice. Thanksgiving sacrifices are offered to God. All is well.

The people rally to their king and ask, "Who are the scum that didn't want Saul *the anointed, the beautiful one,* to reign over us? Let's go find them and kill them to show our loyalty to our new king."

Saul steps in, "Don't act rashly, my countrymen. I hear your willingness to serve me and build the kingdom. Let's celebrate the victory the Lord has given us."

Saul rejoices with the people and wonders what they can see that he can't. He knows he is small and insignificant on the inside. Yet, he is king and loved by many people on the outside. They celebrate him in their midst.

He hears new names from the people as they call out to him as their new king, 'Victorious,' 'Mighty Warrior,' 'Conqueror.' The sweet seduction of being named a leader over a nation is dizzying. It is like warmth to someone who is freezing to death, water to a thirsting soul, air to someone suffocating.

Small nagging questions threaten to rob him of the moment, *What did I do to deserve this? Can the people be trusted? Do they really know who I am?*

He quickly puts the thoughts aside.

For a brief moment, Saul feels alive and enjoys the power of his name. He is loved and adored by many. He accepts the name the people have for him. He decides it is best to hide his feelings of loneliness and insignificance (his shadow) in the love and adoration of the people's name for him.

Chapter VII

Saul and the people are drunk with excitement from their first victory. They take courage and Saul gathers around him 3,000 men as soldiers. He sends the rest of the people home.

A small group of Saul's soldiers, led by Saul's son Jonathan, take courage and attack an outpost of their nearest and biggest neighbor, the Philistines. God is with them and they rout the small army stationed there. The Philistines arise as one army to crush the uprising. They assemble to fight with 30,000 chariots, 6,000 horsemen and more people than can be counted. It is overkill, but that is how they fight and win.

The people of Israel see them coming and realize they only have a few swords among them. When they see their strength in light of the Philistines, they quickly forget God and king and decide to flee for their lives: some to caves, some in thickets, others in cliffs, cellars or pits.

Saul had been told by Samuel during his installation as king, to wait at Gilgal until he came. It was time for Samuel to arrive, but the only thing that had arrived were the Philistines.

Saul *the anointed, the insignificant one,* shouted desperately again, "Where is he? He said he would be here and he is not here. Where is Samuel?"

Those standing around him responded, "No one has seen him sir, he is not to be found."

Saul was nauseous as more and more of his adorers and supporters were fleeing by the second. "Where are they going?" he asked as he pointed to the fleeing soldiers.

"They are going to find a safe place, sir," his assistant responded.

Thoughts terrorized Saul's mind, *The people are fleeing. I will lose my name. I will be insignificant again.*

Saul looked anxiously around, sweat pouring off his face. His brow was heavily creased and his eyes frantic, "Samuel told me to wait for him to come to offer the sacrifice. Then he would give me directions. I don't have any more time. All my people will be gone and I will be dead soon. Get me the sacrifice and I will do it myself."

Saul doesn't care for the people slipping away. He cares only that they represent his name. He has defined and protected himself by their adoration of him and they are now running from him. He will lose the sweet taste of his new name. He will be small and insignificant again. That is a bitter pain to face when you have tasted success and acceptance. He must do something, anything, to keep his new name.

Even if it means going against what God has said?

Yes, even if it means Saul must do what he knows he should not. He must keep his name.

With the pain of the people fleeing him at a time when he needs their help, he wonders, *Maybe it's not good to define yourself by the name others give you. Their acceptance of you is fleeting like smoke in the wind.*

Chapter VIII

Samuel arrives just after Saul offers the sacrifice. He hears of Saul's foolishness and speaks to him, "You acted foolishly and have not kept God's commandment to you. For it was the Lord's desire to establish your kingdom over Israel forever. But now your kingdom will not endure."

It seems a harsh judgment. God's blessing on Saul's leadership is lifted. God searches out a new king, one after God's own heart.

Why?

What's wrong with Saul making a decisive decision to keep the people following after him? After all, he is the king.

It was not the action itself. God is clear that he does not judge us by external things. He looks at the heart.

Leaders are namers God desires to release so they can create a fresh understanding of who He is and what He wants to do. A group's perception is limited and biased, and thus with time grows stale. Although God does not change, a fresh revelation of Him is needed. He brings along a new leader to reveal Himself through. The leader clarifies for the people who God is and His relevance to them. For us, in a constantly changing world, it is an ongoing need for a deepening, refreshing relationship with Him.

What was in the heart of Saul that caused God to limit his influence and length of leadership?

In essence, Saul didn't trust God. He trusted in his own ability and experiences. Another way of saying it is that Saul's view of the world, based on his own experiences and feelings, was the final authority as to what something's name was. He defined himself based on his own feelings, experiences and authority as a namer. This was the one thing God required us *not* to do because He knew the problems we would have. Yet, it is the one thing Saul craves. He wants the freedom and authority to name himself and the people of Israel. He feels he knows best.

God allows that freedom, but Saul and the people must live with the consequences.

Chapter IX

Another victory and more celebration.
God miraculously moves on Israel's
behalf and the enemy flees from them.
Saul's position is gaining power, he
fights more battles and wins.

Position and power are influential and
seductive friends. Saul grows accustomed to dining with them and realizes
this is the way to define himself and
to escape his shadow. He is the king of
Israel, his name is powerful.

With this position and power, he will
prove he is not small and insignificant.
"Saul," Samuel called out.

"Yes, prophet," Saul *the anointed, the
powerful, the insignificant one,* replied.

"The Lord has sent me to tell you He wants you to punish the Amalekites. For they used to sneak up on Israel in the desert and kill the pregnant women and children who were straggling behind. They are completely corrupt and He wants to utterly destroy them. Do not spare any of them or their animals. They are riddled with diseases and sickness. Go, for God is with you," Samuel spoke the word of the Lord for Saul to hear.

Saul gathered his soldiers and heads off to fight.

It is a decisive battle and although Israel wins, Saul loses by disobeying.

God weeps and Samuel joins him. Saul, a leader-namer refuses to submit to *The Sovereign One's* command and thus distorts His image. Samuel goes again to give him the word of the Lord.

"Saul," Samuel called out.

"Blessed are you mighty prophet of God. I have done what God told me to do!" Saul *the anointed, the powerful, the insignificant, the deceived one,* quickly responds.

"Why then do I hear sheep bleating and the sound of many oxen?" Samuel asked.

"The people, they spared the best of the sheep and the oxen, but the rest we utterly destroyed." Saul hesitates and then adds, "The people wanted to give to the Lord the best animals as a sacrifice so we kept them."

Samuel turns to look into Saul's eyes. He sees the fear there. "Let me tell you what the Lord said to me last night. Is it not true that though you were small in your own eyes . . ."

With these words Saul stepped back as if physically hit. Samuel moved closer and continued on, "Though you were small in your own eyes, you were made the leader of the tribes of Israel? God sent you on a mission and told you to utterly destroy the sick, diseased and selfish Amalekites. To completely exterminate them. Why did you not obey the word of the Lord, but instead rushed to get the best things they had to keep for yourself? That was evil in the sight of God."

Saul whined, "I did obey the voice of the Lord. I went on the mission and destroyed the Amalekites, but the people took some of the spoil, sheep and oxen, and they did that so they could give it to God as a sacrifice."

Samuel stood tall and looked into Saul's eyes and declared, "You think you can take from God what you want to build your power and position and to name and thus, protect yourself? That is an abomination. God delights in your accepting your real identity rather than any sacrifice you might wish to buy Him off with."

Saul, cut to the core, confessed, "I have sinned. I didn't completely obey the word of the Lord because I was afraid of what the people would say about me, so I listened to them. But please go with me before the people."

Samuel turned to leave and Saul grabbed his robe and it tore. Samuel declared, "So the kingdom of Israel has been torn from you today."

Saul begged, "I have sinned but please, it is very important to me that you come and honor me before the leaders and people today."

Samuel turned and went with Saul to worship the Lord with the people.

As Saul has defined himself by his position and power, he decides what he wants to do and when. After all, when you have the power and position, you can name who you are and what you should and shouldn't do at will.

Chapter X

What are the consequences we encounter if we transfer our ability to name the world and apply it to ourselves? How does this affect us? How did this affect Saul?

In one word, the consequences are 'insecurity.'

It is like a wind that catches the sails of pride and arrogance we hang from the masts of our heart and pushes us into all sorts of foolishness and evil. Without the winds of insecurity, the heart would not be moved as strongly towards evil.

When we name ourselves based on finite earthly things that change, we become insecure. A name is supposed to confirm who we are. The strength of a name is its clarifying link to unchanging truth. In the depths of our souls we know the only unchanging truth is God Himself. Yet, our shame and guilt shuts us off from Him. In order to avoid the pain of our shame and guilt we determine to make our name meaningful and yet we have lost God's breath in us to do this. In the end we choose things to define ourselves that are continually changing.

Imagine trying to define something by a standard or reference point that is constantly changing. It is impossible. It would be like trying to grab and measure oil with your hands, trying to guide a ship by a lighthouse that is also afloat at sea, or trying to weigh yourself on scales when gravity is changing moment by moment. It will not work. You need unchanging reference points in order to know how to measure or define things. Because *I AM Who I AM*, made us in His image, He put a desire in our heart for a stable, set, unchanging identity: HIS. When that is missing, we become insecure. He never meant for us to question our identity. True security can only come from being named after something that will not change. God is the only one who can fill that role.

Do you still doubt the damage insecurity can do?

Think back to a time you made the wrong choice and got yourself in trouble. Was there a craving to seek evil for its own sake? Or, did insecurity push you to do the things you might not have done without its influence?

Think about lying, stealing, jealousy, envy or hatred. Can you look into these and find the winds of insecurity blowing you into them? I can. The insecurity that wreaks havoc on our soul magnifies the influence of pride in our heart and pulls us with gale force winds towards evil.

Is it any less sin on our part? No. Our heart is proud and arrogant at its center and we must deal with it, but the strength of temptations we face and consequences of our wrong choices do not have to be so severe. Knowing our true name would give us a strength that is not possible when we are insecure. What happens when we base our name on temporal things that change?

What happened to Saul?

He questioned his identity.

He named himself.

He ruled with power and control.

He tried to kill anyone who challenged him.

He became mad.

He forgot his true name.

Thus, he was lonely and afraid, constantly looking for ways to reinforce the name he had given himself and to hide himself from his shadow.

Chapter XI

It is difficult work building a kingdom and Saul needed help to make his position secure. Anytime he saw a strong or talented young man, he would put him into his service. During another battle, Saul was faced with a new crisis. His army cowered on one side of a valley with the Philistines on the other side. The Philistines sent out their biggest soldier, who was over nine feet tall. He was a monster of a man, and they wanted to settle the battle with a fight between their best man and Saul's best man.

No one would dare fight this giant. He would crush them in a minute. A young man stepped forward who was a mere shepherd, cum delivery boy. He was the son of Jesse. David was a ruddy, handsome young man. When he heard of this giant and his challenge, he was shocked and offended that any man or army would stand against God's people.

With rocks in his pouch and his sling-shot in hand, he stepped into the valley and challenged their giant. The giant laughed and mocked the 'child' sent out to fight him. This young warrior ran at him, naming God greater than any giant. The army of Israel watched in disbelief. With sling in hand, in one swift movement, David opened the eyes of all the people as to who God was. He revealed God's name as *Almighty* in their midst.

The Philistines fled and great was the victory that day.

Saul, ecstatic with the new power and his strengthened position, quickly pulled this young man into his service and soon he was a leader in the army. Many successes followed and it was then that Saul heard the women singing, "Saul has slain his thousands, David his ten thousands."

Terror struck Saul's heart. *If David could slay a giant, he could easily slay me. What more can he have now but my kingdom?*

The next two times David appeared before him, Saul grabbed a spear from one of his guards and threw it with all his might at David. He narrowly missed both times. He believed he must kill this young upstart or the power and position by which he defined himself would be taken from him. He would be confronted with his name of being small and insignificant again. David would become the new king and Saul would lose his protection from his shadow.

Relentlessly, Saul pursued David to destroy him. His name would never be secure as long as David lived. He spent the rest of his days hunting David down to protect himself. Every element of his power and position were seized upon and used to gain and keep control over anyone that would challenge him.

There is no peace for those who demand the freedom to name themselves.

Part II

David knew and accepted the identity God had for him and became one of the most influential men in all of Christian history.

How did he become anointed by God? Where did he come from? Surely he had a safe upbringing and was from a good family. Is that what allowed him to understand his identity?

Chapter XII

Samuel spent the night weeping over God's broken heart when Saul demanded the freedom to name himself. Then Samuel was sent to find a young man after God's own heart. A man who understood and lived his life as an expression of God's image.

He showed up at Jesse's house and when he saw Jesse's sons, he knew he had come to the right place. He was ready to anoint, first the oldest and then each of the next six brothers in succession. However, each time God nudged Samuel and reminded him that He was not impressed with the external appearance. Down the line of seven strong and handsome sons Samuel walked, and with each one God said no.

"Do you have any other sons? Because I know I am in the right place and none of these are God's choice," Samuel asked wondering what the problem was. The brothers stared at each other in dismay.

Jesse shifted back and forth nervously and mumbled, "Well, uh, there is one more," and then he stated, "but he is out tending the sheep and can't be here."

Samuel sighed and said, "I have a job to do and I am not going to sit down until he arrives."

Jesse gave the order to a servant and he ran out to get David.

* * *

David ran into the room out of breath and sweating, "Yes father, the servant said I must run as fast as I can to get here. What's wrong?"

Samuel felt the Lord's pleasure in this young man and so he pulled out his horn full of oil and walked over to him and while pouring oil on his head said, "The Lord's anointed." Samuel then turned and walked out.

David *the anointed one*, rubbed the dripping oil out of his eyes and looked at his family with eyes full of questions, "What does this mean?"

The brothers stormed from the room. The oldest yelled back as he left, "You figure it out, runt."

They were at him again. David was the smallest child with seven older, handsome brothers. His father didn't even consider David to be one of his son's worthy of bringing before Samuel when he asked to see his sons. Jesse had just left him in the field and hoped he didn't have to acknowledge him.

Did David take this to heart and struggle as Saul did?

Chapter XIII

It was the same process for both men. Out of nowhere, *The Revealer of Mysteries* steps in and wants to reveal His Name to them and use them as a leader to reveal Himself to the people. We know how Saul responded. How did David?

David had the same roots as Saul. He was the small and insignificant one. He could add to the name his family gave him, rejected. For that is what it appears happened to him. Some argue that David was born through Jesse's involvement with another woman and thus, was the outcast of the family. Maybe he was not planned and came through a wrong relationship Jesse had with a servant. Whatever the cause of rejection, David wrote a psalm about this pain and it reads like this, "I was brought forth in iniquity, and in sin my mother conceived me." It wasn't a theology to him, it was a shadowy pain he carried from his birth. He was born in sin and was not accepted by his family. His name was small, rejected and insignificant one.

That sounds like a painful shadow to run from your whole life. How did he bear the shadow of insignificance and rejection that followed his every step?

Chapter XIV

Solitude is a place few will go to or accept. It is a place where you cannot hide from yourself and it seems a place God sent David while he was still young. When you are all alone, caring for sheep, day after day, your deepest, darkest thoughts have a chance to bubble to the surface. Questions about your identity are never far from your mind.

Have you ever been alone and heard some of your own shadowy thoughts bubble to the surface? For me, they sound like this:

Who am I?

What am I doing here?

Where did I come from?

Nobody cares.

What does it matter? Give up.

I'm not lovable.

In the silence of solitude, David would have heard and felt the pain of his identity and seen his shadow. He could have run I suppose, but where? He had plenty of time to answer the questions about himself. To try and name himself. But he didn't. When we join him, David wasn't afraid of his identity. Somewhere, somehow, David had heard, *I AM Who I AM* calling him and he listened. He had found *The Name Above All Names*.

What does this mean?

In the solitude around him, David felt the pain of his own smallness and insignificance. Added to this was the weight of being a child born into a family that didn't want him. While sitting on a small hill, with darkness surrounding him, he looked at the world and at first glance it only confirmed the insignificance given him by his family. He was the least of his seven strong, handsome brothers, pushed out to tend sheep. He was a pile of dust, on a tiny planet, in a small galaxy, in a vast universe.

In the midst of his struggles to understand himself, I am sure he faced a dilemma.

Should he answer the questions about his identity?

If not, who should?

His shadow?

The feelings of smallness and insignificance within?

The voices of his family that wanted to name him?

The whisper of creation and its Creator?

One thing we know about David was that he was not afraid of pain or struggle. He had the courage to face any enemy. The first one he had to face was within himself. Long before he faced a giant, before a bear or lion challenged him, he had to deal with his own identity and to accept its pain. David embraced it and squarely faced his shadow and still listened, a quality few of us understand today.

* * *

In solitude he watched and listened:
He gazed for hours at the stars and tried to count them by number, but they were too many and too beautiful.

He watched the full moon rise among the trees and then light the night sky and valley around him.

He smelled the grass and sheep as they mingled and became one.

He sensed the sheep looking to him as their shepherd, the one who killed a lion and a bear to save them.

He became aware of his body: learning to run, play music, cast stones, dance, swim and fight. Growing stronger and healing itself when needed. Wonderfully and fearfully made in intricate detail.

He enjoyed the sounds of a dancing brook close by singing simple songs of worship. The sound of the wind dodging and dashing among the limbs of trees. The animals croaking, howling, hooting and growling in the cool of the night.

There was more than just pain to listen to. There was a message. It whispered, danced, swirled and glowed all about him. He felt it in his spirit and listened to *The Sovereign Namer*.

As he listened, poems and songs of worship would well up within him, "O Lord, You have searched me and known me. You know when I sit down and when I stand up. You understand my thoughts from afar. You watch me on the path I am on. You are intimately acquainted with all my ways. Even before there is a word on my tongue, you know it Lord. You circle around me, ahead of me and behind me. I cannot escape from your hand being on me at all times. Such knowledge is too wonderful for me. It is too high, I cannot comprehend it."

At other times, when he would see *The Revealer of Mysteries* at work around him, more songs rose up within him, *"The Sovereign Namer* is gracious and merciful, slow to anger and great in lovingkindness. He is good to all, and His mercies are over all His works."

Solitude became his friend, and as he continued to listen he heard a new name, his true identity. The name God held in trust for him.

I don't know how he came to the place of understanding who had final authority to give him his true identity, I only know that he did. For when we join him, he has found his identity and has an intimate relationship with *The Inti-*

mate One, the only one who truly has authority to answer the question of who we are.

How can I know this?

We can look at difficult situations David faced and see how he dealt with them and how that differs from how Saul dealt with similar situations.

Chapter XV

David had just come back from a battle. He took off his gear and put his sword away. Then he went to report to the king. As he walked into the hall and turned to face the king, a loud thud hit the wall inches from him. A spear stuck in the wall.

Instinctively, he reached for the only weapon he had on him, his sling and slid a stone into the pouch and started swinging it. David turned to find out what enemy had slipped into the king's hall. He saw a man across the hall and just as he was about to let the rock go at the intruder, he noticed the man was Saul. David stopped spinning his sling and stared. It was as if the spear had hit him at the sight of Saul angrily standing there.

"You want my kingdom. You can't have it," Saul *the anointed, the powerful, the insignificant one,* ranted at him.

"My king, I have only come to report a battle won," David *the anointed, The Sovereign Namer's beloved one,* sputtered out.

"I know what is in your heart. You want to be king. You want to take my name and throne from me. You want to challenge me and strip me of my position and power. I won't let you." Saul spit out and reached for another spear.

David quickly ducked out of the hall and fled.

Fled? The next anointed king, warrior and victorious giant killer, fled?

Why would a warrior withhold his weapon in the heat of attack from gaining what he was anointed for?

Joab walked up to David and said, "Why didn't you do it, David?"

David replied, "You mean take his name from him? Or. . ."

Joab interrupted, "Yes, he is power hungry and full of himself. He tried to kill you."

"Or, did you mean establish a name for myself?" David finished his thought.

"You must establish a name for yourself. The only way to do that is to take his name from him. He has no right to try and kill those who have made him successful! You should have stopped his madness," Joab challenged.

"So you think by taking his name I could have established a name for myself?" David asked.

"Of course, that is what it is all about."

David shook his head, "Is it?"

Joab turned and looked David in the eyes, "No one is going to give you a name. You must make it for yourself.

This was your chance. No one would have questioned you for defending yourself against him. Now you will have to flee for your life. With his power, Saul will crush you. What will the people say about who you are now? You will lose your name because you would not position yourself."

David turned away and thought of his days already spent in solitude and seemed to grow in stature. He turned and stood face to face with Joab, eyes ablaze, "I have an identity. It is far greater and more beautiful than a simple title, power or a name given by men. It was gifted to me and I don't need anything else to define who I am. I will not attack God's anointed. I will not destroy, hurt, or cause pain in others to try and justify or distinguish myself. You may strive to earn your name, I will only live to express mine."

Joab turned and muttered as he walked away, "You are crazy. Ideals and fantasy in our world will not get you anywhere. You had better learn that lesson sooner than later."

Chapter XVI

Saul needed power and the people's love in order protect and to keep his name. David loved the people in order to show them God's Name.

David received the love of the people as affirmation and encouragement. The people of the kingdom loved him, the women adored him so much they even wrote songs about him. The men fought next to him and battles were won. Everywhere David went he prospered. Those were good days.

Then Saul heard the women singing and his heart was filled with jealousy. He tried to kill David again and David didn't know what to do. He hadn't done anything wrong.

Finally, upon counsel from his closest friend, Saul's own son Jonathan, he fled for his life to the caves. Alone.

David was not afraid of solitude.

If he demanded the freedom to name himself and defined his name by the people's adoration of him, then when he left, he would have to take them with him in order to keep his name and to protect himself from his shadow. But David was not hiding from his shadow or defining his identity by what the people said.

David knew his place and it was not defined by the people's adoration. It was a gift given him from *The Giver of All Good Things*. Nothing or no one could take that from him.

Whether David was alone in a dirty cave or killing the biggest, baddest giant around, it did not define who he was, for his value came from the One who created him.

Chapter XVII

Times and seasons pass and so they did for David. He went from soldier to cave dweller. He fled for his life among the caves and worried not about kingdoms, but food and survival.

But as the anointing of God must give birth, so David's leadership came forth. Saul and his sons were killed in a battle and David was anointed the new king. More battles were fought and won and the Nation of Israel was firmly established.

Times and seasons have their own temptations and struggles, it was no exception for David as the established leader of the Nation of Israel.

* * *

It is a hard job being king. Battles to be fought and won. People to talk with, decisions made, a kingdom to be run. David was a good king and cared about his people.

However, the load got very heavy. Day after day of struggle and grind.

Even though David had accepted his identity from *The Name Above All Names*, many of those he worked with hadn't.

Being a namer among a group of people who are constantly raising questions of their own identity and seeking to name themselves is a constant challenge. For those who don't know their position, it is often the most difficult task in life. Leaders carry the brunt of this struggle as many of the followers then look to the leader instead of God to get their name.

* * *

"My king, you are invited to a banquet given to honor those who support you," David's assistant began.

"Another one? I have been to too many this month. I grow weary of them." David *the anointed, The Sovereign Namer's beloved, the uncomforted one,* groaned.

"Yes my lord. There are many who struggle to get your presence at their party. You do know what your presence means to them, don't you?"

"Humor me, why should I go?"

"If the king shows up at their party, their name is associated with yours. They are known as friends of the king. They establish a name for themselves as your friend."

"That is the reason I must attend these parties?" David said in a quandary.

"My king?" the assistant responded, not knowing what to say.

"I know it is not your fault they seek to make their name through using my position. I am not the answer, yet they expect me to be. It just wearies me. Put it on the schedule and I will attend," David stated and the assistant left to organize the day.

Just as his assistant was leaving his minister of trade entered and asked, "My king, may I have a moment of your time."

"Yes, go ahead," David said as he sat down.

"Your son is causing problems again. This is my job. I am in charge of over-seeing the traders who come and go in the city. My name is on the line and your son keeps giving traders permission to trade in the city that I have not authorized," the minister of trade said sharply.

"Your name is on the line?" David asked.

"Yes, you have given me my title. You have put me in this special place. You have given me directions to keep order in the city. I am doing my best but your son keeps usurping my name among the people."

"Is your name your title? I have given you your name?"

The minister of trade looked up at David not knowing how to respond.

David saw the look and replied, "Send my son in and I will talk with him."

"Thank you my king. I will cause you no problems. You can be assured I will represent your name well," with that the minister of trade left.

As he was leaving his assistant appeared and said, "Sir, an official from the king of the Ammonites is here to see you."

"Send him in," David ordered.

The official appeared and greeted the king, "King of Israel, thank you for giving of your busy time to see me. I truly appreciate your willingness to listen to a request from my king."

"You're welcome, how may I help you?"

"Well, my king has sent me to ask a favor of you. It is well known by all the kingdoms around that you have found favor with God. He has been with you and given you victories that most of us have only dreamed of. You are highly esteemed and we value our relationship with you. It seems a king to the east of us is plotting against us and we need to establish a stronger name so that they will fear us. We, at least right now, cannot do this on our own. We ask that you would help us to do this. Would you come and bring gifts to our king?"

The official lowered his voice and almost whispered, "We will pay you very handsomely for this service. If we could show our neighbors that your name is linked to ours, we could stop a war from happening."

David took a deep breath. "I appreciate your desire to stop a war. I will help as I can. I will send my sons to your kingdom with gifts. There will be no charge for this as I do value your friendship and stopping a needless war."

The official bowed with his head almost to the ground and said, "Thank you, oh king. Truly your name is great. I will tell my king of your splendor. Thank you." With that he left.

David's assistant appeared, "Joab says they are going out to fight some raiders and as it is your custom to go, he wanted to make sure you would join them."

David held up his hand. "Tell Joab, I am not going anywhere. I do not want to meet with anyone else. I am weary, no I am beyond weary, of people and their attempt to name themselves by me. This nameless world wears me down and I have had enough. I am going for a walk."

The assistant nodded and left.

David rose and went to find his blessed solitude. In order to catch the cool evening breeze, he went for a walk on the roof of the palace. As he walked he pondered over his day. *I am so weary of people and their demands on me. If only I could take a break. Oh, Lord, it is so tiring to be a namer in a nameless world. They question their identity, but they don't want to walk through the pain and find their identity in you. They just want to use the identity you have given me as they attempt to name themselves. It tires me to the bone.*

With a gentle breeze cooling him off he peered over the side and found himself looking down into a house where a beautiful woman is bathing. He stares and stares, too tired to fight and protect himself from the comfort he feels he needs.

Soon, the desire grows to find comfort and a lame thought enters his head. *He should tell this woman to put up some blinds to protect others from seeing her. He must call her to come up to see him so he can tell her to get blinds.* Soon they are in bed together and David has discredited his identity and *The Desire of All Hearts'* name.

* * *

Was it because he wasn't married or couldn't find the right wife? No, he had many wives and he could have had more. It wasn't about sex. As king he could have had all the sex he wanted. It was about the pain of being a namer, in a world that will suck you dry because you know your identity. It was about false comfort.

The pain of knowing your identity in a nameless world can be overwhelming. So many nameless people around you clamor for you to help them by giving them a little part of yourself. It is like working in a country struck by a famine where everyone is starving. You have something to give but it can't possibly meet all their needs.

Remember, you can't give people their identity, only *The Father of Life* can do that.

Chapter XVIII

"Ittai?" David *the anointed, the Sovereign Namer's beloved, the forgiven one,* called out. "What are you doing leaving with us? You only arrived yesterday. You are a foreigner and in exile here. Shall I make you wander with a king who has no throne? I am not even sure where I am going. All I have left is my honor. Go join the new king."

"David" Ittai responded, "God is with you. I will go with you."

"Come then and join us as we flee," David sighed.

Ittai turned away and then turned back and looked at David, "May I ask a question, my king?"

"Yes, but be warned. I have more questions than answers myself."

Ittai looked at the ground and then up to the regal old man standing before him, "Why? Why are you fleeing before your son who has no right to your throne while you are strong? Why flee?"

David watched hundreds of his followers pass by as they fled the city. Many dressed in fighting armor, others dressed in their best attire, each bowing before him as they passed. "That is a question that I have struggled with myself. Absalom has decided that he has to make a name for himself. He has taken it upon himself to get power to establish his name. The only way he can do that is to take my position."

He hesitated and then continued, "I am a warrior. It would be much easier for me to fight. But then I ask myself, fight for what? My kingdom? It isn't mine, it is God's. There is one thing I have learned over the years. If you use power to get a name," David took a deep breath, "Or to keep a name, the name is not worth having. I already have an identity that far exceeds my position. My desire is to guard the integrity of that identity."

David looked into Ittai's eyes and asked, "Now it is my turn to ask a question of you for part of the answer to your question lies in yourself. Why would you follow an old king who must flee from his son who is seeking to make a name for himself and steal the throne? I have nothing to give you but trouble."

Ittai grinned, "That is an easy answer, my king. A throne does not make a king. Power does not make a king. Who you are at the core of your being is what makes you a king. I have heard far and wide of your humility and would gladly follow any man, be he poor, a slave or a king, when he bears the image of God as you have done."

With that they turned together and fled the city.

Chapter XIX

Along the path of life there is one Sage we all must seek for help. One who understood the challenges that Saul and David faced. One who understands the challenges you and I face. His name is Authority.

"I am confused. Can you help me?" I called out.

"Yes," Authority replied.

"Why are you so important?"

"I am the resource that all finite creation needs."

"What do you mean?"

"Each year, each month, each day, actually with each decision, you are confronted with your own limitations. You are finite and you don't know what is the best choice to make."

Authority hesitated for a moment and then leaned over and whispered, "You are not God so you don't know what to do. You need help and so you want to find out who knows what to do and listen to them."

"OK," I replied, "I can see without any problem that I am finite. And just so that you are aware, I know I am not God. But I do not understand what you mean by saying that I am looking for authority. Authority to me is just a position and I don't care that much about a position."

"When I say you are looking for authority. I mean that you are looking for something or someone who knows who you are and what is real. In essence, they know something you don't and you trust them and listen to them. Another way of saying it, is that what you give authority to will determine what you see."

"What do you mean when you say authority will determine what I see? My eyes don't change when authority changes, do they? Can you give me some examples because I don't see clearly enough how this is important with naming myself or the world around me."

"You are right in saying that your eyes don't change. But seeing and identifying is so much more than the mechanics of how eyes work. The eyes just send signals to your mind. It is your mind that interprets the signals sent to it based on who or what it recognizes as having authority."

Authority hesitated and then continued, "Okay, here is an example. A small group of cells is growing quickly in a women's uterus. Is it named 'tissue' that can easily be removed because of its inconvenience to the host, i.e. the woman? Or, is it named 'a child,' a human being that is made in the image of God that will live forever and will never be duplicated again?"

"Ohh, so," I said as I thought out loud, "if I say my emotions have the final say or have authority, then when I don't feel like keeping the baby, I can name it as pre-baby tissue and thus remove it? If I say God has the final say and thus authority, then when He calls it a baby, even if I feel differently, I name it in line with what He says because I submit to His authority to know what is real?"

"You catch on quickly," Authority said encouragingly and continued, "I will give another example. Two different people groups look upon a desert and see the same thing but interpret it very differently. One group considers the land to be cursed and it was Allah's will to be barren. Since Allah has all authority and they could no more change Allah's will than the movement of the sun, they live under the curse, accepting their due from him and do nothing to change it.

On the other hand, the other group considers the land given to them by God as a blessing. They see themselves as his overseers who are to watch over it. They consider it their responsibility to protect it and make the best use of it. They divert water, plant many different kinds of fruit trees and even forests. After a short while they harvest their work and the land produces abundance."

I nodded my head and spoke my thoughts out loud, "Their view of God and how His authority works determined how they saw themselves and what they were to do. We all see the same world, but based on who or what has authority, we interpret it differently. As you gave that example I thought of sand. One person holds it in his hand and sees it as a waste. Something to be swept up and thrown away. Someone else sees it in a new way and creates glass. A transparent substance that can be seen through and yet blocks out the wind and cold weather. Someone else sees the sand and creates the basis of a silicon computer chip. The foundation of modern technology. I have never seen it this way before!"

"You must think very clearly about authority for it is the basis for how you will see and name all of life!" Authority stated.

"I have a wild thought. If this is true, could you say that all resources begin in the mind?"

"Yes, that is exactly right. But my question is *whose* mind?"

"Oh, I see what you mean," I hesitated as the thought hit me, "Whose ever mind I trust, will be the place I look for resources. It may be that I limit myself to my own mind, or to my mother or father, my family or even my culture. I will then look to these people for resources. However, if I submit to God's authority, then all resources begin in His mind and I will seek Him for help."

I took a breath and then asked, "One more question. How does this apply on a personal level?"

"What do you mean?" Authority replied.

"Well, I have strong feelings and experiences from my family and culture that have given me a name from the very earliest memories. I get images of a tough guy who can do anything floating around in my head, therefore a name I have for myself is tough and independent. I have experiences of people saying to me, 'You will never amount to anything' and I submit to their stated authority. That experience defines who I name myself to be. How can I deal with that?"

"Those are very real experiences and images that we are given as we grow up. I won't deny that. But there is a difference between experiencing something and interpreting it. How we interpret an experience depends on who has final authority. If I want to have final authority, then I have the final say as to what the experiences mean. If a good God does, then I have to yield to His greater understanding and seek Him for what those experiences mean."

"So even on a personal level, it all boils down to who I will trust to know best my identity and thus my true name?" I pondered.

Authority nodded his head, "That's right. To find the one who should have authority you look for who is the wisest, most powerful and who genuinely wants what is best for you. When you find that person, you will have found someone who has true authority."

Part III

There is one who came to reveal the Namer to us. He was *The Son of The Sovereign Namer* and the very expression of the Namer in our midst. He came to reveal *The Sovereign Namer* to us and give us back our name.

Chapter XX

Then Jesus was cast into the wilderness to be tempted by the devil. And after He had fasted for forty days and forty nights, He became hungry.

The tempter spoke first, "If you are *The Son of The Sovereign Namer*, prove it. You are hungry, you're dying from lack of food. If you truly have the identity you say you do, all you have to do is prove it. Name these rocks, bread. That will prove who you are."

Jesus answered him and said, "It is written, by naming rocks, bread, it will not prove my identity. Man shall not live by proving he has a name, he shall live by the identity God has spoken for him. What identity God speaks is answer enough."

Then the devil took Him into the holy city, and had Him stand on the pinnacle of the temple, and said to Him, "If you are *The Son of The Sovereign Namer*, prove it. We are standing before your people. They will give you any name you want if you will step from here and not be hurt. For it is written that 'God will give his angels protection concerning you and on their hands they will bear you up, Lest you strike your foot against a stone.'"

Jesus said to him, "On the other hand, it is written, 'You shall not force God to do something just to make Him prove what your identity is.'"

Again, the devil took Him to a very high mountain, and showed Him all the kingdoms of the world and their glory and he said to Him, "I know you are *The Son of The Sovereign Namer*. All these things I will give to you if you take the easy way of expressing your identity. After all, you will get these things eventually. I am just offering them to you in a much easier manner. All you have to do is name me a Sovereign Namer."

Then Jesus said to him, "Get out of here Satan! For it is written, 'There is only one *Sovereign Namer* and he alone is worthy of all praise. He alone establishes an identity and is worthy of my expressing His identity in the way that best honors him."

Then the devil left Him and angels came and ministered to Jesus.

Chapter XXI

Evil was smothering the land. Like a woman in childbirth, pain and agony were bringing forth life in the midst of darkness. Those standing around the cross cowered and moved closer to each other as the sun failed in the middle of the day.

"What is happening?" one whispered to another.

"It is Jesus. It is because of who He is. He is the first man to have the same name and identity. He revealed that we do not know our name and we could not bear it," another whispered back.

Jesus, *The Son of The Name Above All Names*, bowed His head and said, "It is finished," and with those words, He gave up His spirit.

A New Name was revealed in that moment. It was a name that was a part of God's heart from the beginning. Man's selfishness gave God the opportunity to reveal Himself in a new way. There on the cross, Holy, Blameless, Sovereign and Humble, bearing the sins of the world in His heart, Jesus bore our punishment in His body and revealed the new name, *The Lamb of God* who takes away the sins of the world.

Death clung to him, screaming and clinging with all its might. It held him for three days. Yet, even death could not stop the power of His name. During these three days Jesus went to Hell and started there to declare our true identity. Our name would be our identity.

What was the name? Listen and see if you can hear it.

"I AM Who I AM," Jesus' voice announced his presence. He then declared the new Name of God, "The Lamb of God who takes away the sins of the world."

Darkness cringed and found no place to hide. Howls arose from the deepest darkest places as the name was spoken forth. From among the ashes and darkness, faintly at first, one by one, voices began to arise like sparks into the night sky.

"Here I am. I knew you would come."

"Here I am over here. I am bound and can't get up."

"Yes, I hear you, I am stuck and can't move. Say your name again."

"I know that is you Jesus, I would know your voice anywhere."

"It is time. I knew you would come. I am ready."

Jesus listened carefully to each one and then declared, "Those who know my voice. Those who have turned from their selfishness. Those who have submitted to my authority. All those who have loved and desired My Name."

There was a ripping sound like cloth being torn in two. Jesus defeated the shadow of sin that fell across all mankind and spoke forth our true name.

"SONS of *The Most High Father*, COME FORTH."

"DAUGHTERS of *The Most High Father*, COME FORTH."

Light broke forth for the first and last time in that place. Most of the creatures cried out in agony and fled under rocks to hide. Those who knew the voice arose to accept their names and join the Family of God. Sons and Daughters of *The Most High Sovereign Namer*.

On the third day Jesus confronted and conquered another shadow. Death was defeated once and for all.

With the keys of death and hell in his hand, Jesus went to his disciples.

He spoke to them, "All authority to define the identity of mankind is restored to me. Therefore, go and tell every deceived and rebellious namer, *The Father of Life* is not mad at them for their foolishness. He has found a way to give them back their true name. One based on who He is, not on who they are. Go and call them forth saying:

"SONS of *The Most High Father*, COME FORTH."

"DAUGHTERS of *The Most High Father*, COME FORTH."

"And as you go, I will be with you until the end of time."

Epilogue

It was now the end of all time. The agony, pain, suffering and drama of our world was over. All humanity gathered together on a broad plain before the throne of God. The sea gave up the dead which were in it, from the bowels of the earth the dead were brought forth, even death and Hades gave up the dead which were in them; and all the dead, the great and the small, were gathered together. All who had ever lived and held the breath of life were there.

Jesus carried a large book out and laid it on the altar that was before the throne. It had written on its cover, 'The Book of Life.'

Jesus stood before the book and called out, "This book is our family book. If you have accepted Our name and been adopted into Our family, then your name will be in here. Let Me say this clearly so you understand. If you are a son or daughter of *The Most High Father*, if you have accepted My Father as your Father, if you have accepted Our name for you, then We have placed your name in The Book of Life. It is now time for the roll call to be made for the family of God. When you hear your name called, you may come forth."

With those words Jesus slowly opened The Book of Life. Time seemed to stand still as He began to read out the names of those who were written in it.

Those whose names were not found in The Book of Life were thrown into the lake of fire.

About the Author

Matt Rawlins was born on the West Coast and grew up in a Christian home. He jokes that his earliest prayer was "Lord, help me not to swear." It seemed clear to him that if you didn't swear, you were a good person and if you were a good person, you could avoid hell and go to heaven. After all, wasn't that the purpose of heaven? To avoid hell?

In his late teens God began to stir his mind and he remembers sitting with his family around a dinner table and asking, "What is love?" It seems that question led him in desperation to find out if there was a real source of love or if the world was just a bad dream.

It was through this searching that Matt ended up doing a training program with Youth With A Mission (YWAM). He recalls, "One time when I was crying before God, words came to me that seemed to sum up my whole life. The words were 'I'm so lonely, I'm so lonely.' It was then that I realized Christianity was a relationship of love and not fear. I guess it was then that I realized how much Jesus loved me and I fell in love with him."

He volunteered with YWAM and spent three years working in Saipan, Micronesia. From there, he went on to Hong Kong where he met his beautiful wife, Celia, (she is from Hawaii) and they were married. After a year in Hong Kong they moved to Singapore to take over the YWAM work there. Their son, Joshua was born there. They were in Singapore for five years.

Later they moved to Oregon where Matt's family was living, and Matt went back to school. He finished his BA in Management and Communications and his Doctorate in leadership development and communication.

Currently the Rawlins family lives in Kailua - Kona, Hawaii. He also works with University of the Nations and is involved in training and teaching all over the world in leadership development.

Interested in More?

Amuzement Publications produces a series of books that captures the hearts of readers and provokes them to 'Muze' over who God is, who they are and the part they are to play in the world around them.

The Question
Is God good to all?
Who God is and how we view Him
is The Question we are all confronted
with. The story moves through creation
and explores the devil's attack against
God's character. It focuses on Job's
struggle with The Question and finishes
with how God answered The Question
through Jesus and in His coming final
judgment.

The Namer
God created us in His image. A primary
part of that is our ability to give meaning to the world around us by naming
it. The only limitation God placed on us
was that we could not name ourselves.
When we took that on through our
rebellion against Him, we can see the
troubles and difficulties it caused in our
world. The story follows Saul and David
and looks at how they named themselves and the challenges they faced
because of that.

Emails from Hell

Executive emails from below. How to bring down a leader and an organization.

This book is a take off on C. S. Lewis' work. Explore the bent wisdom of a senior demon as he tries to train a young demon in the art of using his subject (a leader) and his organization to accomplish their own purposes.

Mysteries Beyond the Gate and other peculiar short stories

A collection of short stories that deals with working together in unity called 'The Dance,' hardship called 'The Craftsman,' giving our gifts to God called 'The Song,' dealing with bitterness called 'Raising a Grudge,' and many, many more.

The Container

God made man complete in himself and yet incomplete alone. Why? As an expression of being made in God's image, He wants us to learn to build deep, lasting relationships that will provide a place for Him to dwell. This 'container,' that our relationships build, is the challenge that all families, groups, communities and organizations face. The story looks at our struggles as we work to build a container for God to dwell in.

Redicovering Reverence

The path to intimacy. What is reverence? How can it be a foundation for intimacy? Can we be intimate without it? These and many more questions are answered in this practical and yet stirring look at the beauty of reverence and it's place in our walk with God.

Printed in the United States
26249LVS00005B/25-27